Only five notes are needed to start this book:

Remember to hold the recorder with the left hand at the top.

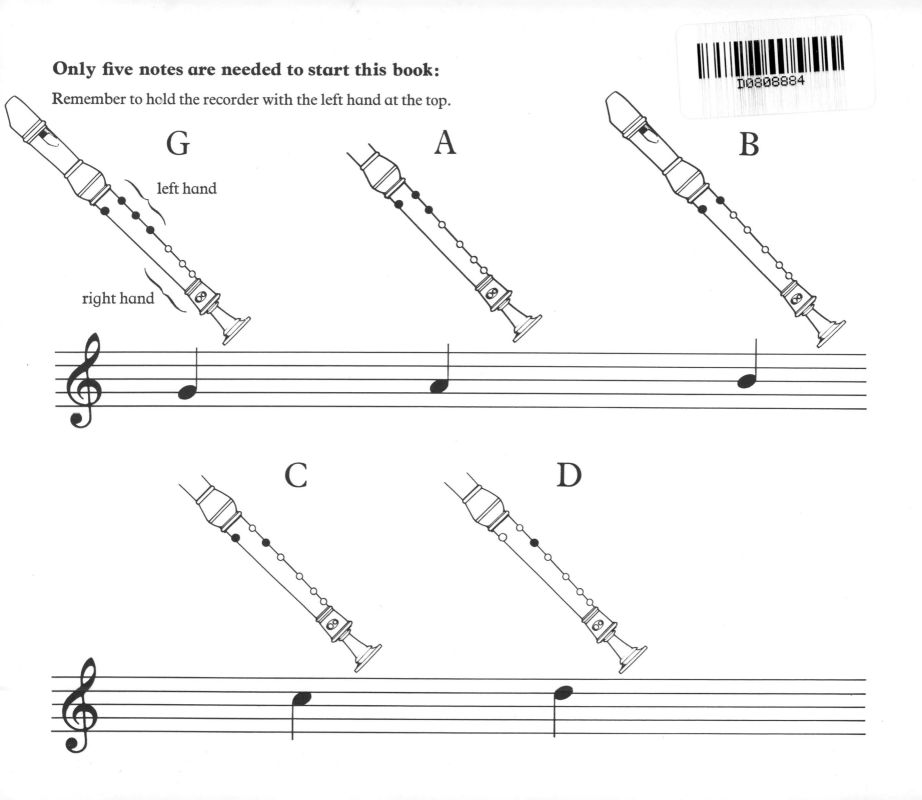

G

left hand

right hand

A

B

C

D

1 When the saints go marching in

spiritual
Ta-ra-ra boom-de-ay 29 (in F)

recorder

G B C D

Oh   when   the   saints

tuned percussion

with cymbals and drum

go   marching   in,   oh when the   saints   go

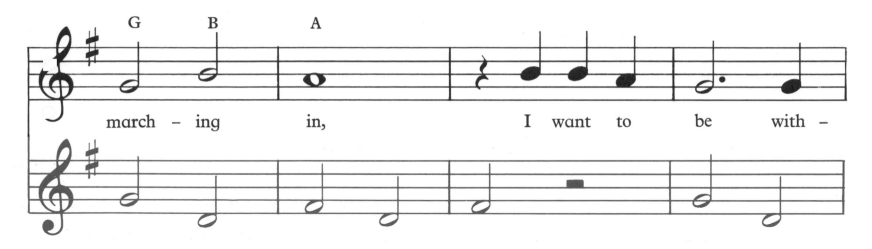

march – ing   in,   I   want   to   be   with –

in   that   num – ber _____ when   the

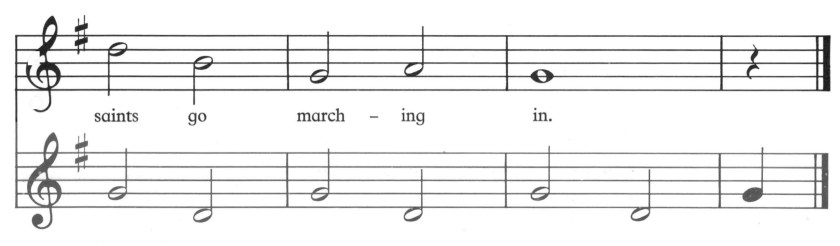

saints   go   march – ing   in.

2 Andrew mine, Jasper mine

words: C.K. Offer
music: Moravian carol tune
Carol gaily carol 28

Indian bells: play at each ❋

slow and gentle

An-drew mine, Jas-per mine, Ti-mo-thy and A - bel,

Hur - ry to Beth-le-hem, to the com-mon sta - ble.

There you'll find a ba - by small, sleep-ing in a swaddling shawl,

On your way, on your way, To our Sa-viour born to - day.

3 Old woman, old woman

traditional
Apusskidu 10

Old wo - man, old wo - man, will you come a shear - ing?

Speak a lit - tle loud - er, sir, I'm ve - ry hard of hear - ing.

4 Dance of the cuckoos

Marvin Hatley

woodblocks: etc.

tick tock tick tock

5 Shepherds' hey

Morris dance tune

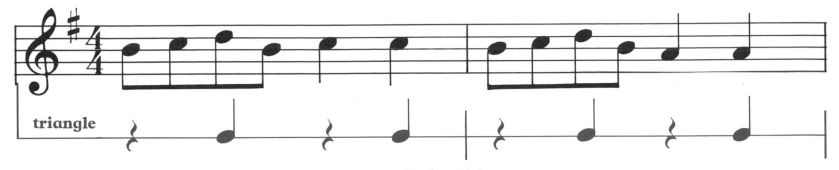

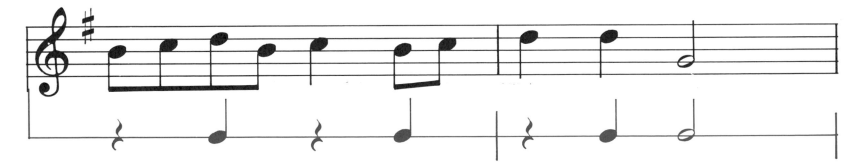

triangle

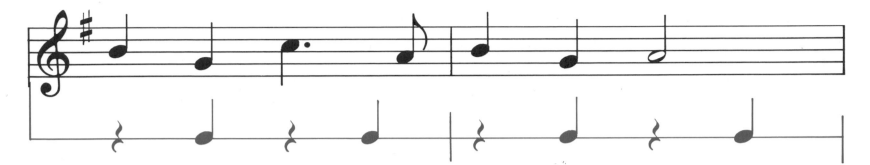

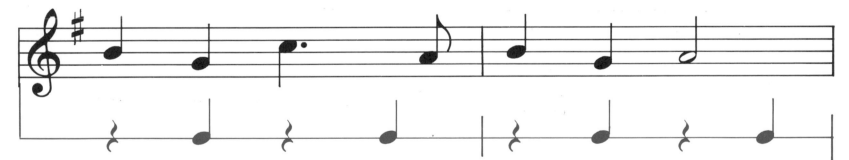

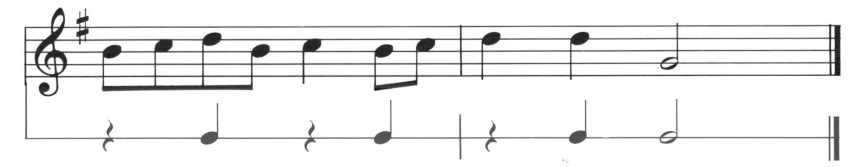

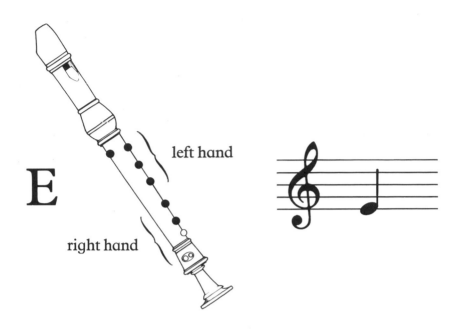

E

left hand

right hand

6 Annie's song

John Denver

You fill up my sen - ses, like a

E

night in a fo - rest, _____ like the moun - tains in

spring – time,   like a   walk   in   the   rain, _____

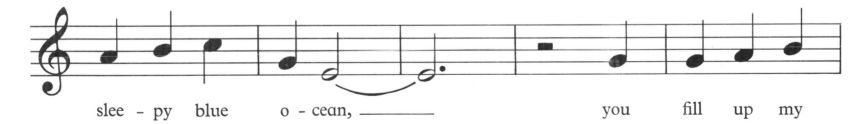

like a   storm in the de – sert,   like a

slee – py blue   o – cean, _____   you   fill   up   my

sen – ses,   come   fill   me a – gain. _____

low D

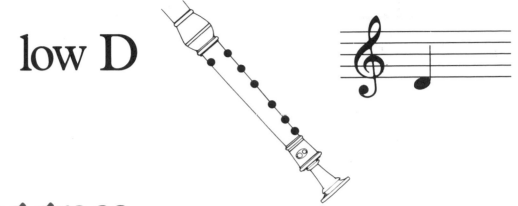

7 Amazing grace

words: John Newton
music: traditional
Ta-ra-ra boom-de-ay 28 (in F)

A - ma - zing ____ grace, how ____ sweet the sound that ____

saved a ____ wretch like ____ me. ____ I ____

once was ____ lost but ____ now am found, was ____

blind   but _____ now   I   see. _____

8 The gypsy rover

Leo Maguire
The Jolly Herring 37

The   gyp - sy   ro - ver   came   o - ver   the   hill

bound   for   the   val - ley   so   sha - dy,   He

whis - tled   and   sang   till   the   green   woods   rang,   and

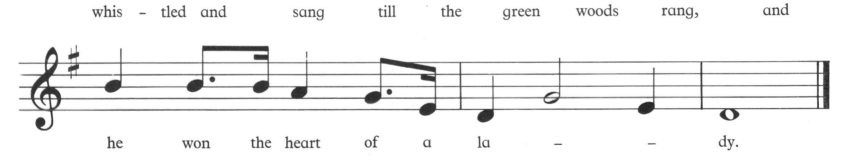

he   won   the   heart   of   a   la - - dy.

9 The Skye boat song

traditional Scottish

slow and flowing

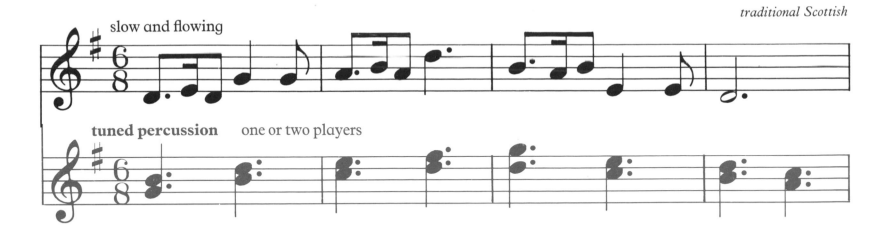

tuned percussion   one or two players

Fine

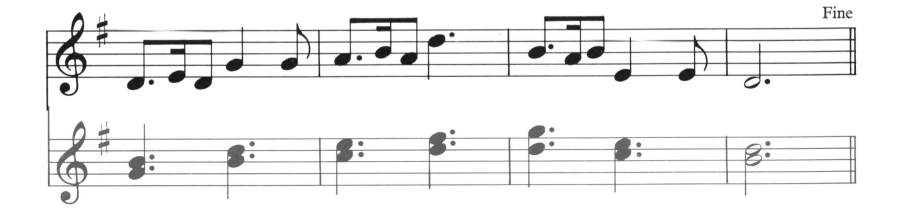

D.C. al Fine

"D.C. al Fine" means go back to the beginning and repeat as far as "Fine".

In the first section the lower notes of the tuned percussion part also make a second recorder part, using only five notes.

The second section is stormier, more urgent, than the first – a cymbal accompaniment could be improvised here. Use different tuned percussion instruments for the two sections.

F♯

Lord of the dance has F♯ in the key signature, marked at the beginning of each line:

top line is high F

bottom space is low F

This means <u>all</u> Fs must be played as F♯s.

10 Lord of the dance

words: Sydney Carter
music: traditional
Someone's singing Lord 29

I danced in the morning when the world was be - gun, and I

percussion

player 1

(had my birth)

player 2

danced in the moon and the stars and the sun, and I came down from heaven and I

Percussion: Four players, with player 2 echoing player 1 in the first half of the song and player 4 echoing player 3 in the chorus. The note patterns can be varied. Use two pairs of contrasting instruments: dance-linked ones like tambourine, castanets, tambour or Indian bells would be suitable.

11 Winds through the olive trees

This sign ⸙ marks suitable breathing points.

traditional French
Carol gaily carol 37

Winds through the o – live trees soft - ly did blow _____
round lit - tle Beth – le - hem, Long___ long a – go.

chime bars (A, D)

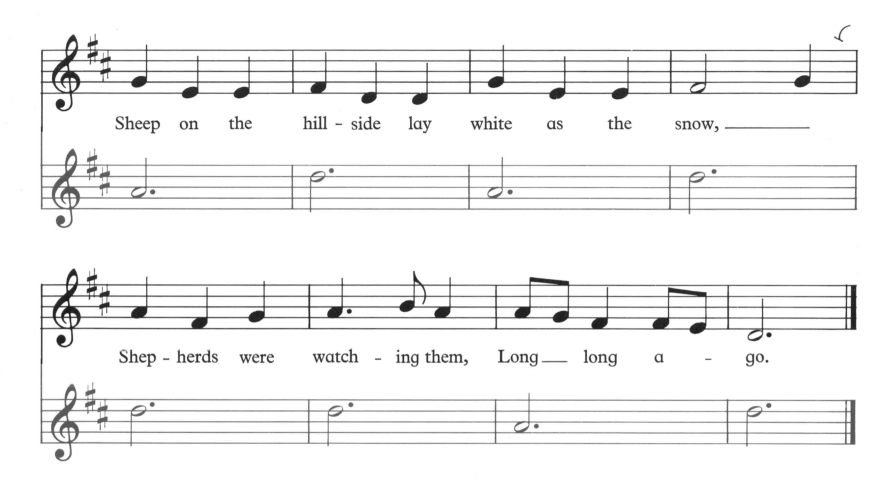

Choose where to breathe, don't just carry on till you run out of breath. The words, as well as the breathing marks, will help you choose the best breathing places.

ostinato for tuned percussion:

12 Infant holy, infant lowly

words: E. M. G. Reed
music: traditional Polish
Carol gaily carol 14

In - fant ho - ly, in - fant low - ly, for his bed a cat - tle stall,

tuned percussion (B, C′, D′, E′)

ox - en low - ing, lit - tle know - ing Christ the babe is Lord of all.

Swift are wing - ing, an - gels sing - ing, Nowells ring - ing, ti - dings bringing,

Christ the babe is Lord of all, Christ the babe is Lord of all.

13 Michael, row the boat ashore

spiritual
Ta-ra-ra boom-de-ay 30

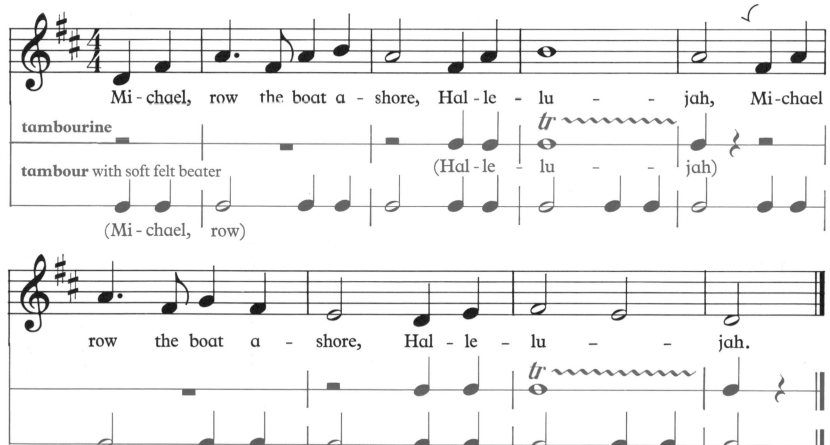

Mi - chael, row the boat a - shore, Hal - le - lu - jah, Mi - chael

tambourine

(Hal - le - lu - jah)

tambour with soft felt beater

(Mi - chael, row)

row the boat a - shore, Hal - le - lu - jah.

14 I saw three ships (first tune)

traditional

triangle (play at each ❊)

tuned percussion or **piano**

I saw three ships come sail - ing in, on Christ - mas day, on Christ - mas day, I saw three ships come sail - ing in, on Christ - mas day in the morn - ing.

15 I saw three ships (second tune)

traditional

tuned percussion
one or two players

I saw three ships come sail - ing in,

sail - ing in, sail - ing in, I saw three ships come

sail - ing in, on Christ - mas day in the morn - ing.

16 Row row row your boat (4-part round)

traditional
Flying a Round 27

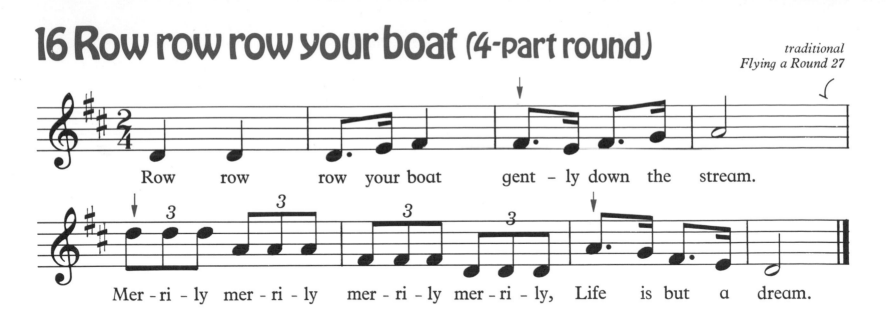

Row row row your boat gent – ly down the stream.

Mer – ri – ly mer – ri – ly mer – ri – ly mer – ri – ly, Life is but a dream.

↓ Each arrow marks the point at which a new part can enter.

If possible use tenor recorders as well as descants.

17 Whose pigs are these (4-part round)

traditional
The Jolly Herring 64

Whose pigs are these? Whose pigs are these? They are John Potts', you can

tell 'em by the spots, and I found 'em in the vi – ca – rage gar – den.

18 Kum ba yah

traditional
Someone's singing Lord 23

triangle (play at each ✳)

tuned percussion
one or two players

Kum ba yah, my Lord, kum ba yah, Kum ba

yah, my Lord, kum ba yah, Kum ba yah, my Lord, kum ba

yah, O Lord ___ kum ba yah.

19 Last night I had the strangest dream

Ed McCurdy
Alleluya 45 (in C)

Last night I had the strang – est dream I e – ver

triangle

dreamed be – fore. _____ I dreamed the world had

all a – greed to put an end to war. _____

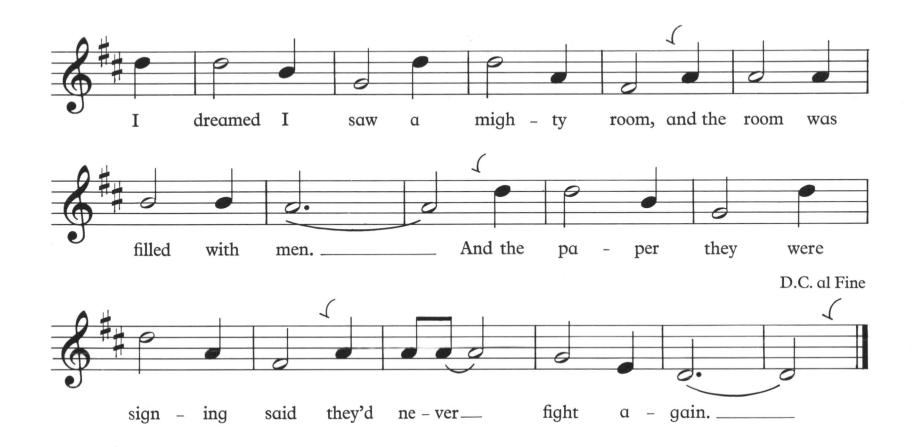

I dreamed I saw a migh – ty room, and the room was filled with men. _____ And the pa – per they were sign – ing said they'd ne – ver __ fight a – gain. _____

D.C. al Fine

Percussion

For the second part of the song, choose a contrasting
instrument, and work out a suitable pattern for it to play.

20 If you're happy

traditional
Apusskidu 1

If you're hap – py and you know it clap your hands. If you're

hap – py and you know it clap your hands. If you're

hap – py and you know it then you'll sure – ly want to show it, if you're

hap – py and you know it clap your hands.

Percussion

Two players on tuned percussion, one for the bass notes :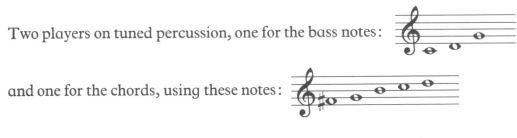

and one for the chords, using these notes :

plus a tambourine player, whose part is marked by asterisks : (✳)

21 Daisy Bell

Harry Dacre
Apusskidu 8 (in F)

2nd descant recorder or tuned percussion

Dai — sy, Dai — sy,

give me your ans – wer, do. _____ I'm half

cra – zy, all for the love of you. _____ It

22 Clementine

traditional
Apusskidu 12

tuned percussion

Oh my dar – ling, oh my dar – ling, oh my

dar – ling Cle – men – tine, thou art lost and gone for –

– e – ver, dread – ful sor – ry Cle – men – tine.

23 Under Bethlehem's star so bright

traditional Czech
Carol gaily carol 38

Un – der Beth –lem's star so bright, Shepherds watched their flocks by night.

tuned percussion (D, F♯, A, D′)

tambourine

etc.

Hy – dom hy – dom, tid – li – dom, hy – dom hy – dom tid – li – dom.

Acknowledgements

We are most grateful to all the teachers and advisers who have helped us to prepare this book. Our particular thanks to Leonora Davies, Oliver James, Catherine Johnson, Martin Sheldon and Cynthia Watson.

The following copyright owners have kindly granted their permission for the reprinting of words and music:

Box & Cox Publications Ltd for 8 'The gypsy rover'.

TRO Essex Music and The Richmond Organization for 19 'Last night I had the strangest dream', ©Kensington Music Ltd, ©1950 (renewed 1978), 1951 (renewed 1979) and 1955 Almanac Music Inc.

Evans Brothers Ltd for the words of 12 'Infant holy, infant lowly'.

Interworld Music Ltd/Winter Hill Music Ltd, 15 Berkeley St, London W1 for 6 'Annie's song', ©1974 Cherry Lane Music Co.

Oxford University Press for the words of 2 'Andrew mine, Jasper mine'.

Southern Music Publishing Co Ltd, Southern Music Publishing Co (Australasia) Pty Ltd and Southern Music Publishing Co (S.A.) Pty Ltd for 4 'Dance of the cuckoos', ©1932 Southern Music Publishing Co Inc. Liber-Southern Ltd, 8 Denmark St, London WC2.

Stainer & Bell Ltd for 10 'Lord of the dance'.

Every effort has been made to trace and acknowledge copyright owners. If any right has been omitted, the publishers offer their apologies and will rectify this in subsequent editions following notification.

Printed by Caligraving Limited, Thetford, Norfolk